The Cooking Pot

Retold by Jonathan Shipton

Illustrated by Allan Curless

Once upon a time an old woman went to town. It was market day.

The old woman saw a big cooking pot on one of the stalls. 'I wish I had a pot like that,' she said. 'But I have no money.'

Just then a man came over.
'I am Tom,' he said. 'Why are you so sad?'
'I would like that cooking pot,' said the old woman. 'But I have no money.'

'I have no money to give you but
I will help you if I can,' said Tom.
'Thank you,' said the old woman.

So Tom went up to the stall.
He said to the man on the stall,
'Do your pots have holes in them?'
'No, they do not,' said the man.

'But if I did find a hole,
what would you do?' asked Tom.
'I would give you something from
my stall,' said the man.

So Tom looked at all the cooking pots.

Some were little...

some were big...

and some were very big.

'This is a good pot,' said Tom.

'Yes,' said the man.

'And this is a good pot,' said Tom.

'Yes, it is,' said the man.

'And this is a very good pot,'
said Tom. 'But it has a hole in it.'
'A hole in it?' said the man.
'My pots don't have holes in them.'

'Yes, they do,' said Tom. 'Have a look.'
And he gave the pot to the man.
The man looked all over the pot
but he could not find a hole.

'Look **in** the pot,' said Tom.
So the man looked in the pot
but he could not find a hole.

'No, not like that,' said Tom.
'Like this.'
And he put the pot over
the man's head.
'You see,' said Tom. 'It has a hole
in it as big as your head.'

'Now you must give me something from your stall,' said Tom.

The man was very cross but he said, 'Yes, I will. What do you want?'

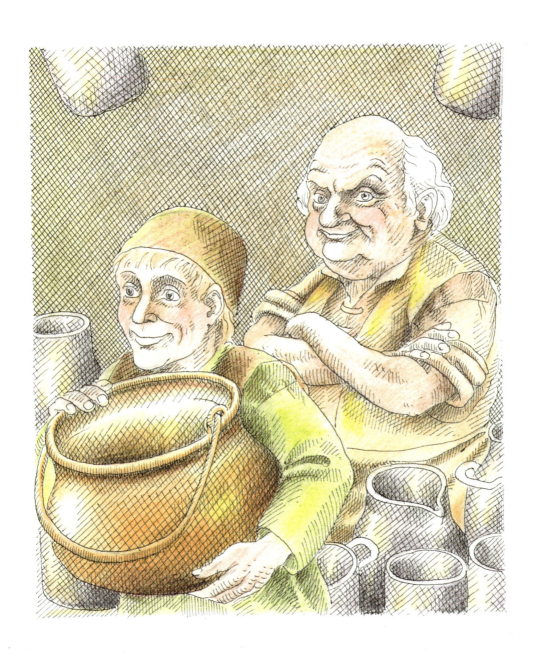

'I want this,' said Tom, and he walked off with the big cooking pot.

Tom gave the pot to the old woman.
The old woman was very happy.
'Thank you, Tom,' she said.
'Thank you for my cooking pot.'